Four Corners

Jack C. Richards · David Bohlke

with Kathryn O'Dell

Workbook

CAMBRIDGE UNIVERSITY PRESS
Cambridge, New York, Melbourne, Madrid, Cape Town,
Singapore, São Paulo, Delhi, Tokyo, Mexico City

Cambridge University Press
32 Avenue of the Americas, New York, NY 10013-2473, USA

www.cambridge.org
Information on this title: www.cambridge.org/9780521127677

© Cambridge University Press 2012

This publication is in copyright. Subject to statutory exception
and to the provisions of relevant collective licensing agreements,
no reproduction of any part may take place without the written
permission of Cambridge University Press.

First published 2012

Printed in Hong Kong, China, by Golden Cup Printing Company Limited

A catalog record for this publication is available from the British Library.

ISBN 978-0-521-12769-1 Student's Book 4A with Self-study CD-ROM
ISBN 978-0-521-12770-7 Student's Book 4B with Self-study CD-ROM
ISBN 978-0-521-12766-0 Workbook 4A
ISBN 978-0-521-12767-7 Workbook 4B
ISBN 978-0-521-12765-3 Teacher's Edition 4 with Assessment Audio CD / CD-ROM
ISBN 978-0-521-12763-9 Class Audio CDs 4
ISBN 978-0-521-12756-1 Classware 4
ISBN 978-0-521-12762-2 DVD 4

For a full list of components, visit www.cambridge.org/fourcorners

Cambridge University Press has no responsibility for the persistence or
accuracy of URLs for external or third-party Internet Web sites referred to in
this publication, and does not guarantee that any content on such Web sites is,
or will remain, accurate or appropriate. Information regarding prices, travel
timetables, and other factual information given in this work are correct at
the time of first printing, but Cambridge University Press does not guarantee
the accuracy of such information thereafter.

Art direction, book design, photo research, and layout services: Adventure House, NYC

Contents

7 New ways of thinking **49**

8 Lessons in life **57**

9 Can you explain it? **65**

10 Perspectives **73**

11 The real world **81**

12 Finding solutions **89**

Credits

Illustration credits

Kveta Jelinek: 52, 58, 69, 84; Andrew Joyner: 62, 70, 76; Greg Paprocki: 79, 92; Garry Parsons: 59, 67, 83; Rob Schuster: 68; Richard Williams: 51, 63, 73, 91

Photography credits

49 ©Gail Baker/SureWest; 50 ©Emir Rifat Isik; 53 ©Elena Elisseeva/Alamy; 55 (top to bottom) ©Caro/Alamy; ©The Bridgeman Art Library/Getty Images; 56 (top to bottom) ©Media Bakery; ©Shutterstock; ©Shutterstock; ©D. Hurst/Alamy; 57 ©Media Bakery; 60 ©Alamy; 65 ©Istock Photos; 66 ©James Porto/Getty Images; 70 ©Jamie Cooper/SSPL/Getty Images; 71 ©Ryan Cheng/Getty Images; 72 ©Shutterstock; 74 (all) ©Media Bakery; 80 ©Bravo/Everett Collection; 85 (top to bottom) ©Media Bakery; ©Radius Images/Alamy; ©Media Bakery; ©Shutterstock; ©Media Bakery; ©Shutterstock; ©Brownstock/Alamy; ©Media Bakery; ©Brownstock/Alamy; 86 ©Garry Gay/Alamy; 88 ©Photo Library; 93 (top row, left to right) ©Jim West/Alamy; ©Yellow Dog Productions/Getty Images; ©Lana Sundman/Alamy; (middle row, left to right) ©Adrian Sherratt/Alamy; ©David Cordner/Getty Images; ©Media Bakery; (bottom row, left to right) ©Superstock; ©Tony Anderson/Getty Images; 96 ©John Moore/Getty Images

unit 7

New ways of thinking

A Inventions

1 Put the letters in the correct order to make adjectives. Then write the negative forms with *in-* or *un-*.

1. t n c e n o e v i n   convenient   inconvenient
2. e n i c t o n n a l v o
3. f s i i a n c n i t g
4. g i n v i m t a i a e
5. i c r e v a e t
6. u l c u c e f s s s
7. v e c f e i f e t
8. v e e f u t l n

2 Complete the text with the word in parentheses or its negative form.

Today, people think answering machines are ___inconvenient___ (convenient) because they are used to voice mail. But when Willy Müller made the first automatic answering machine in 1935, it was a ___significant___ (significant) invention. In 1960, the Ansafone, invented by Dr. Kazuo Hashimoto, was the first _____ (successful) answering machine sold in the U.S. It was followed by the PhoneMate in the 1970s. However, many of these early answering machines were _____ (effective) because they were so big and heavy! Then a man named Gordon Matthews changed everything. Matthews was an _____ (imaginative) man who looked at things in new and _____ (conventional) ways. In 1979, he started VMX, the company that made the first voice mail system. Voice mail is _____ (effective) because you can listen to your messages using your phone. The system is more _____ (convenient) than an answering machine.

Ansafone

Unit 7   Lesson A   49

3 Put the words in the correct order to make sentences.

1. great / a / is / designer / My sister / such / .
   My sister is such a great designer.

2. creative / She / so / is / .
   _____

3. Her / are / interesting / ideas / so / .
   _____

4. She / she decided to open / that / imaginative / so / is / her own store / .
   _____

5. online store / good / a / such / idea / was / Her / .
   _____

6. It / successful / her other job / that / she quit / was / so / .
   _____

7. ten people working for her / is / a big company / that / she has / such / Now it / .
   _____

8. She / I / hardly ever see her / that / busy / so / is / .
   _____

4 Complete the conversation with *so* or *such*.

Dennis: Hey, Laila. Did you see that list of cool ideas for cell phones on the Internet the other day? It was ____such____ an amazing list.
₁

Laila: No, I didn't see it.

Dennis: Well, some of the ideas were _____ creative, and there was _____ a cool picture of one of them, too.

Laila: Tell me about it.

Dennis: Well, it was _____ a great idea. It was a cell phone that is only five square centimeters.

Laila: That's _____ small!

Dennis: Yes, it is. But it opens and gets bigger! It was _____ an imaginative idea that the inventor won an award for it.

Laila: Wow. I love new inventions. The list sounds _____ interesting . . . What's the website?

50 Unit 7 Lesson A

5 Rewrite the sentences with *so* or *such* in the correct position.

1. Wow! That salesman is enthusiastic about the Easy Broom.

    Wow! That salesman is so enthusiastic about the Easy Broom.

2. But it looks like an ineffective product!

    _____

3. The inventor's idea is unimaginative.

    _____

4. His design is conventional.

    _____

5. He'll have a difficult time getting people to buy it.

    _____

6 What do you think of the invention in Exercise 5? Write your own opinion with some of the words in the box. Use *so* or *such*.

convenient / inconvenient	design
creative / uncreative	idea
significant / insignificant	invention

Example: *It's so creative, but it's such an insignificant invention.*

_____

7 Make one sentence. Use *so . . . that* or *such . . . that*.

1. That new phone is popular. There aren't any left in the store.

    That new phone is so popular that there aren't any left in the store.

2. Daniel is creative. He won an award for his idea.

    _____

3. Eva is a successful businessperson. She got two promotions this year.

    _____

4. That new car is cheap. I might be able to buy it.

    _____

5. The Internet is a great invention. People all over the world are using it.

    _____

B Got any suggestions?

Read the pairs of questions and responses. Complete each conversation with the correct pair.

| Do you have any ideas? One idea could be to invite her. | Got any ideas? One solution might be to keep it in the refrigerator. | ✓ Got any suggestions? Something we could try is to put them on top of each other. |

A. Hee Jin: You have such a big book collection!

Debbie: I know. There isn't room for all of the books on my bookshelf.
Got any suggestions?
                1

Hee Jin: _____
                         2

Debbie: What do you mean?

Hee Jin: You know, instead of standing them up, put them on each other, like this.

Debbie: Oh, I see. Good idea.

B. Lydia: Hey, my cell phone isn't working.

Josh: Oh, no. What are you going to do?

Lydia: Hmm . . . I don't know. _____
                                                                      1

Josh: _____
                          2

Lydia: That's a weird idea. Why?

Josh: Well, it really works. But it only keeps the phone working for a while. You'll probably have to get a new one soon.

C. Mario: Hey, do you want to go to a concert on Friday?

Hank: Yes! But I can't. I have plans with Jill.

Mario: But it's our favorite band . . . The Pines.

Hank: Oh, no! I have to go. But what about Jill?

Mario: _____
                          1
_____
                          2

Hank: That's a good idea. I think she'll like the band, too. Thanks!

C Accidental inventions

1 Circle the correct words to complete the texts.

Something New to Eat!

The **invention** / invented of the ice cream cone was an accident! It was **invention** / **invented** in 1904 at the World's Fair in St. Louis, Missouri. Arnold Fornachou's ice cream stand was such a **success** / **succeeded** at the fair that he ran out of dishes. Next to Arnold, Ernest Hamwi was selling waffles – a flat type of cake. When Arnold ran out of dishes, Ernest rolled one of his waffles and **creation** / **created** a dish. Ernest put the ice cream in the waffle. This **innovation** / **innovated** became the ice cream cone!

After the fair, Ernest Hamwi **development** / **developed** a new company that sold ice cream in waffle cones. His company **success** / **succeeded**. The **design** / **designed** has changed over the years, but waffle cones are still popular.

A New Color

In 1856, William Perkin was a young scientist. He **introduction** / **introduced** a new dye to the world – by accident! Dyes are used to change the color of cloth. Perkin was trying to make a new medicine, but by accident he made a beautiful purple dye. Perkin's dye was the first that was not made from a plant or an animal. It was an **improvement** / **improved** over other dyes because it was less expensive and easier to make. The dye **proved** / **proof** to be successful. Perkin's **creation** / **created** was also a new color. He called it *mauve*.

2 Answer the questions with your own information.

Example: <u>I designed a tree house for my yard. My parents helped me make it.</u>

1. Have you ever designed anything? What was it? _____
2. What's your biggest success in life? _____
3. What do you think is the best invention in the past ten years? _____
4. Have you ever been asked for proof of who you are? When? _____

3 Circle the correct phrase to complete each sentence.

1. The crossword puzzle _____ by Arthur Wynne in 1913.
   a. is invented   (b.) was invented   c. have been invented

2. At first, Arthur's puzzle _____ a word-cross.
   a. is called   b. was called   c. have been called

3. Crossword puzzles _____ in newspapers for about 100 years.
   a. is printed   b. was printed   c. have been printed

4. The first crossword puzzle book _____ in 1924.
   a. is made   b. was made   c. have been made

5. Today, some crossword puzzles _____ online.
   a. are done   b. were done   c. have been done

6. *The New York Times* newspaper _____ for its crossword puzzles. Many people buy the newspaper because they want to do the crossword puzzle.
   a. is known   b. was known   c. were known

4 Complete the text with the correct form of the verb in parentheses. Use the passive form of the simple present, simple past, or present perfect.

www.history/inventions/cup.com

Fun facts about the zipper

- The zipper __was invented__ (invent) in 1913 by Gideon Sundback.
- It _____2_____ (call) the "Hookless Fastener" for over ten years. Then, in 1925, it _____3_____ (name) the zipper. A person using a zipper on a boot said "zip" because that was the sound that it made. It _____4_____ (call) the zipper ever since that time.
- Zippers _____5_____ (use) today on all types of clothing. In the past, they _____6_____ (use) on clothing for people in World War I.
- Zippers _____7_____ (made) of metal since 1913. Today, many of them _____8_____ (made) of plastic.
- Pants with zippers _____9_____ (wear) by men for many years, and they still wear them today. But women's clothing did not have zippers until about 1930. Then zippers _____10_____ (put) on women's clothing, too.

5 Write sentences with the words in parentheses and the passive form of the simple present, simple past, or present perfect.

1. (Today, / car windshields / make / of glass)
   Today, car windshields are made of glass.

2. (Windshield wipers / invent / in 1905 by Mary Anderson)
   _____

3. (The design of windshield wipers / improve / since 1905)
   _____

4. (Windshield wipers / put / on the front of cars / for many years)
   _____

5. (Today, / windshield wipers / find / on the front and the back of some cars)
   _____

6 Rewrite the sentences in the passive form.

1. Alexander Graham Bell invented the telephone.
   The telephone was invented by Alexander Graham Bell.

2. People have used telephones since 1876.
   _____

3. Someone made the first cell phone call in 1973.
   _____

4. 1.4 billion people used cell phones in 2003.
   _____

5. Over 4.6 billion people use cell phones today.
   _____

6. People develop new kinds of cell phones every year.
   _____

D Making life easier

1 Read the text. Then number the items in the order they were invented.

_____ refrigerator   _____ vacuum cleaner   _1_ sewing machine   _____ microwave

Remember when?

Many inventions make life easier. We forget what life was like before these things were invented. Here are some inventions that made life easier at home.

The Refrigerator   The refrigerator was invented in 1876 by Carl von Linde. Before that, many people had icehouses. They bought ice and kept it in a building outside of the house. People put their food in the icehouse to keep it cold and fresh. But the icehouse didn't keep things fresh for long. The refrigerator makes keeping food fresh much easier.

The Vacuum Cleaner   Before the vacuum cleaner was invented, people used brooms to clean their floors. The first vacuum cleaner was invented in 1860 by Daniel Hess, but it was very heavy. One person had to move the base of the machine, and another person moved the part that picked up dirt and dust. Many people improved Hess's design, but vacuum cleaners were still expensive and heavy. In 1908, James Spangler made an effective and less expensive vacuum cleaner. After that, people started buying them for their homes.

The Sewing Machine   Imagine not being able to buy clothing in a store! Before the invention of the sewing machine, everyone made their clothing at home by hand. Many people tried to invent a sewing machine in the 1800s, and Elias Howe invented the first useful sewing machine in 1846. Others followed. The invention of the sewing machine allowed companies to make large amounts of clothing that could be sold in stores.

The Microwave   The microwave was invented by accident. Percy Spencer was working with radar waves at his job. The radar waves cooked a candy bar that was in his pocket! This gave him an idea, and he created the microwave oven in 1945. The first microwave was called the Radar Range. It was used mostly in restaurants.

2 Read the text again. Then rewrite the sentences to correct the underlined mistakes.

1. Carl von Linde invented <u>the microwave</u>.   _Carl von Linde invented the refrigerator._
2. You needed only <u>one person</u> to use the first vacuum cleaner.
   _____
3. <u>Daniel Hess</u> made a cheaper vacuum cleaner. _____
4. Before sewing machines were invented, people made their clothes <u>in stores</u>.
   _____
5. The first microwave was called the <u>Percy Spencer Oven</u>. _____

56 Unit 7 Lesson D

Lessons in life

unit 8

A Why did I do that?

1 Write new words with the correct prefixes. Add *dis-*, *mis-*, or *re-*.

1. judge ____*misjudge*____   4. think _____
2. continue _____   5. regard _____
3. spell _____   6. make _____

2 Complete the conversations. Use the words in the box with the correct prefixes: *dis-*, *mis-*, or *re-*.

| agree | consider | do | ✓like | pronounce | understand |

A. **Carla:** Let's go to a Tom's Hamburgers for lunch.
   Dae Ho: I'd rather not. I ____*dislike*____ red meat.
                                    1
   Carla: Really? Please _____ .
                                    2
   They have good salads there, too.
   Dae Ho: Oh, OK. We can go to Tom's, then.

B. **Mary:** This painting is beautiful!
   Jill: I _____ . I think it's ugly!
                     1

C. **Claire:** I'm sorry. I didn't mean to _____ your name.
                                                    1
   Sean: That's OK. It's hard to say. You say, "Shawn," but it's spelled S-E-A-N.

D. **Mr. Ito:** Did you _____ the directions, Kelly? Your homework
                                1
   is completely wrong.
   Kelly: I understood the directions, but I think I did the wrong page.
   Can I _____ it?
              2
   Mr. Ito: OK. Give it to me tomorrow.

Unit 8 Lesson A 57

3 Complete the conversation with the past perfect of the verbs in parentheses.

Sheila: How was the movie with Amanda last night, Felipe?

Felipe: The movie was OK, but I was really embarrassed. I started to pay for the movie, but I realized I _had left_ (leave) my money at home.

Sheila: So, did Amanda pay for the movie?

Felipe: Yes, she did. I _____ (also / forget) to turn off my cell phone before we went into the theater. My mom called!

Sheila: Did you answer it?

Felipe: Yes. The movie _____ (not start / yet), so I went outside. When I got back, it _____ (already / begin).

Sheila: Oh, no!

Felipe: Then I realized I _____ (not bring) my glasses, so we moved to the front of the theater. It was really uncomfortable.

Sheila: I'm sure Amanda didn't mind.

Felipe: I don't know. I emailed her. I checked an hour ago and she _____ (not respond / yet).

4 Write sentences with the words in parentheses. Tell what Kim *had* done and *had not* done by the time the guests arrived for her party. Use the past perfect with *yet* or *already*.

1. (Kim / not take out / the garbage)   _Kim hadn't taken out the garbage yet._
2. (she / wipe off / the kitchen counters)   _She had already_ _____ .
3. (she / wash / the dishes) _____
4. (she / do / the laundry) _____
5. (she / not hang up / the clothes) _____
6. (she / go / grocery shopping) _____
7. (she / not put away / groceries) _____
8. (she / not make / the pizza) _____

5 Write sentences with the words in the chart. Use the simple past and the past perfect in each sentence.

Happened first	Happened second
1. Ms. Jones / mispronounce / my name	she / ask / me how to spell it
2. she / know / his brother for two years	Sandra / meet / Jake
3. Jackie / call / her dad ten times	she / heard his message / on her voice mail
4. we / already / ask / him a lot of questions	we / agree / to John's idea
5. he / think about it / carefully	Hai / disregard / Tim's advice
6. the company / borrow / a lot of money	it / close

1. _Ms. Jones had mispronounced my name_
   before _she asked me how to spell it_ .
2. By the time _Sandra met Jake_ ,
   _____ .
3. _____
   before _____ .
4. By the time _____ ,
   _____ .
5. Before _____ ,
   _____ .
6. _____
   before _____ .

6 Write sentences with your own information. Use the past perfect and simple past.

Example: _I'd taken English classes before I began this class._ or
 I hadn't taken English classes before I began this class.

1. (not) take English classes / before / begin this class
   _____

2. (not) thought about other cultures / before / start studying English
   _____

3. (not) often misspelled English words / before / take this class
   _____

4. (not) mispronounced a lot of English words / before / practice them in this class
   _____

5. (not) read my email / by the time / do my homework last night
   _____

Unit 8 Lesson A 59

B *I'm sure you'll do fine.*

1 Complete the conversation with the sentences from the box.

> Do you have a list of their names?
> ✓ Hi, Tia. How are you?
> I know Mandarin. I can help you.
> I'm pretty nervous about it.
> Really? That would be great!
> Well, I don't want to mispronounce their names.
> I'm sure you'll do fine tomorrow.

Chao: *Hi, Tia. How are you?*

Tia: I'm OK, I guess. But people are coming to my office tomorrow from China, and _____

Chao: Really? Why?

Tia: _____

Chao: _____

Tia: Yes, I do. Why?

Chao: _____

Tia: _____

Chao: We'll practice tonight, and _____

2 Complete the conversations with phrases for expressing worry and for reassuring someone.

A. **John:** I have to meet Sue's parents tomorrow, and I'm kind of
   worried about it .
             1

   Mark: I'm s_____ .
             2

B. **Mi Yon:** I have an English test tomorrow, and I'm a little
   a_____ .
             1

   Brenda: D_____ .
             2

   E_____ .
             3

C What if...?

1 Complete the chart with *get* or *make* and the correct phrases from the box.

| ✓ a big deal | an effort | mistakes | out of | rid of things |
| a fool of myself | into trouble | on my nerves | over it | up my mind |

get . . .	make . . .
	make a big deal

2 Complete the email with expressions with *get* and *make*. Use the simple present.

Subject: Oh, no!

Hi Sharon!

How are you? I'm OK, but I need some advice. I'm having a problem with my roommate. Jack _gets on my nerves_ (1) a lot. First of all, he's very messy. He never _____ (2) he doesn't need. I try not to _____ (3) about it, but I might have to say something. No one is perfect. We all _____ (4), but I would just like him to _____ (5). You know, try a *little*!

Oh, and he always tries to _____ (6) doing the chores. I wash the dishes, I take out the garbage, and I even hang up *his* clothes! I know I should try to _____ (7) and disregard his behavior. He's a really nice person. He lent me $100 last week and said it was no problem. What's your advice? I have a hard time with decisions, and I can never _____ (8). I don't want to say the wrong thing.

What should I do?

Write soon!

Ian

Unit 8 Lesson C 61

3 Read the sentences. Then answer the *yes / no* questions. Use short answers.

1. If Dana had listened to her parents, she wouldn't have gotten into trouble.

   Did Dana listen to her parents?   <u>No, she didn't.</u>

   Did she get into trouble?   _____

2. If Carlos had made up his mind, he would have a new car right now.

   Did Carlos make up his mind?   _____

   Does he have a new car?   _____

3. If Paul had said he was sorry, Carolina would have gotten over it quickly.

   Did Paul say he was sorry?   _____

   Is Carolina still upset?   _____

4. Mona wouldn't have made a fool of herself if she hadn't sung so loudly at the party.

   Did Mona sing loudly?   _____

   Did she make a fool of herself?   _____

5. Vicky would have understood the homework if she hadn't been late for class.

   Was Vicky late for class?   _____

   Did she understand the homework?   _____

4 Circle the correct forms to complete the conversation.

Hiro: Hi, Lydia. Did you and Kyle get home OK last night?

Lydia: Not really. It took us over an hour.

Hiro: Really? Didn't you drive home?

Lydia: Well, if I (**hadn't dropped**) / **wouldn't have dropped**₁ my keys out the window by mistake, we **had driven** / **would have driven**₂ home.

Hiro: Oh, no! Did you look for your keys?

Lydia: Yes, but we couldn't find them. We probably **had found** / **would have found**₃ them if it **hadn't been** / **wouldn't have been**₄ so dark.

Hiro: So, did you take the bus home?

Lydia: No. If we **had left** / **would have left**₅ earlier, we **had taken** / **would have taken**₆ the bus. But it was too late, so we walked home!

62   Unit 8   Lesson C

5 Complete the story. Change the main clause of the last sentence to an *if* clause in the next sentence.

If I hadn't gone to the concert, I wouldn't have seen Julia.

1. <u>If I hadn't seen Julia</u>, she wouldn't have gotten on my nerves.
2. <u>If she hadn't</u> _____, I wouldn't have made a fool of myself.
3. _____, Julia would have invited me to her party.
4. _____, I would have talked to Brenda.
5. _____, I would have asked her to dinner tonight.
6. _____, I wouldn't have had a boring night watching TV alone!

6 Look at each picture. Then write a third-conditional sentence about it with words from the box.

| buy the computer | get rid of some things | have room for the sofa | rain |
| forget her credit card | go to the baseball game | ✓pass the test | ✓study |

1. <u>If she had studied, she would have passed the test.</u> or <u>She would have passed the test if she had studied.</u>

2. _____

3. _____

4. _____

D A day to remember

1 Read the text. What three types of memory are mentioned?

_____   _____   _____

What will you remember?

Patricia Sanders remembers the day she met her husband perfectly. It was over 50 years ago. She remembers that it rained the day that they met in a bookstore. She remembers he was wearing a blue raincoat, and she was wearing a red dress. She even remembers what he said to her. But she can't remember what she had for lunch today.

The brain has different ways to store memories. It stores some information in short-term memory, which can only keep the information for about 30 seconds. For example, if you look up a phone number, you can store the number in your brain long enough to make the phone call. But a minute later, you might forget the number. The brain also stores information in what some people call "recent memory." This allows you to remember what you had for lunch or what you did yesterday. Important information is stored in long-term memory. Some information is stored in long-term memory after you repeat it a lot. For example, if you call the same phone number over and over again, your brain will remember it for a long time. If you read one book on a subject, you may forget a lot of it. But if you read several books and articles about the subject, you will remember the information for a lot longer. Significant events are also stored in long-term memory. So a year from now, you might forget what you had for lunch today, but you will remember the first time you met your husband or wife or got a promotion at work.

Research shows that it's natural for people to have recent memory loss as they get older. People often experience this memory loss after the age of 50. So, it's normal that Patricia remembers the day she met her husband. It's in her long-term memory. And it's normal that she can't remember what she did yesterday. Her brain's recent memory is not working as well as it used to. Some people have severe memory loss, but Patricia's problems are normal.

Tips to help with "recent memory" loss:

- Make a list of things you want to remember.
- Take medicine at the same time every day.
- Put your keys in the same place every day.
- Don't make a big deal about forgetting things. Relax, be honest, and laugh about the problem.

2 Read the text again. Answer the questions.

1. What has Patricia forgotten? _what she had for lunch today_
2. How long can the brain store information in short-term memory? _____
3. What kind of memory stores information that is repeated often? _____
4. Which type of memory is it normal for older people to lose? _____
5. How could an older person remember to take his or her medicine? _____

Can you explain it?

A Everyday explanations

1 Add *-less* or *-ful* to the word in parentheses to complete each sentence.

1. I just broke my cell phone. Now it's _____useless_____ (use)!
2. I got _____ (meaning) information from Dr. Jacobs. I think I will be healthier if I follow her advice.
3. A lot of trees fell last night in that _____ (power) windstorm.
4. Benny and Tom went bungee jumping. They're _____ (fear)!
5. Laura is such a _____ (care) driver. She always drives too fast.
6. Air pollution is _____ (harm). It can make you sick.
7. I don't know how to help you. I feel so _____ (power).
8. Penny has a big dog, but it's _____ (harm). It won't hurt you.
9. Mr. Garcia's explanation was very _____ (use). I finally understand algebra!
10. You can borrow my computer, but please be _____ (care) with it.
11. Sue is very _____ (fear) of animals. She won't even go to a zoo!
12. That question was completely _____ (meaning). No one knew how to answer it.

2 Write your own ideas.

1. Two things that are useful for school: _____a computer_____ and _____
2. Two things that are harmful to the environment: _____ and _____
3. Two things you should be careful doing: _____ and _____
4. Two people who are fearless: _____ and _____
5. Two meaningful classes you have taken: _____ and _____
6. Two inventions that are useful: _____ and _____

3 Complete the webpage with past modals of the verbs in parentheses.

www.localmysteries/cup.com

KimKim: Last night I saw a strange light in the sky. Did anyone see it? What could it __have been__ (be)?
1

DonRJ: The city might _____ (have) some fireworks.
2

Rita86: Fireworks make noise. It was too quiet last night. You couldn't _____ (see) fireworks.
3

QT007: I saw the light, too. I think something could _____ (fall) from an airplane.
4

CindyT: It couldn't _____ (come) from a plane. Look at the picture . . . It's going *across* the sky, not *down*.
5

WhyMe: OK. KimKim must _____ (take) this picture with her camera open for a long time. I'm sure she's kidding!
6

* * *

PeteOP: Did anyone hear a strange noise on Main Street last night? I think it might _____ (be) a wild animal!
7

Jeff1982: You couldn't _____ (hear) a wild animal, PeteOP. There aren't any wild animals around here.
8

4 Complete the sentences with past modals. Use *must, couldn't,* or *could* and the correct form of the verb in parentheses.

1. I don't know why Patricio wasn't in class today. He __could have been__ (be) sick.

2. Tracey was at a concert last night, and she saw her favorite band. I'm sure she _____ (have) fun!

3. Jackie _____ (drink) milk. She can't have dairy at all.

4. My sister hasn't called me all week. She usually calls me every day. I wonder if she _____ (lose) her cell phone.

5. I've been waiting for Tonya at the airport for an hour. I'm sure her plane _____ (leave) late.

6. Marianna is really good at math. She _____ (got) a bad grade on the test.

7. Oh, no! My mother _____ (try) to call me. My cell phone has been off, and there's a missed call. She always calls me at this time.

5 Why wasn't Larry in class yesterday? Complete the sentences with past modals. Use *must*, *couldn't*, or *might* and the correct form of the phrases in the chart.

	Not sure	Sure
Steve	be sick	be at home
Clara	go out with friends	not stay at home
Diana	miss the bus	have a good reason
Ken	watch the baseball game on TV	forget about class
Tina	go to a job interview	need to miss class
Mr. Anderson	think there was no class	not check the class schedule

1. Steve thinks Larry _might have been sick_ .
   He _must have been at home_ because his car was there.

2. Clara thinks Larry _____ .
   She says he _____ because she went to his house after school, and he wasn't there.

3. Diana thinks Larry _____ .
   She says he _____ for not coming.

4. Ken thinks Larry _____ .
   He says Larry _____ .

5. Tina thinks Larry _____ .
   She says he _____ .

6. Mr. Anderson thinks Larry _____ .
   He says Larry _____ .

6 Look at each picture. Write what you think happened. Use past modals.

Example: _She must have broken her arm._

1. She _____ .

2. She _____ .

3. He _____ .

4. He _____ .

B I'm pretty sure that . . .

1 Complete the chart. Write the sentences from the box in the correct column.

> But it's likely that there is water on Mars.
> But it's very probable that some kind of life was there.
> ✓ I doubt that people ever lived on Mars.
> I'm pretty sure that there used to be trees on Mars.
> It's highly unlikely that there were trees on Mars.
> Well, it's doubtful that I would ever get the chance.

Expressing probability	Expressing improbability
	I doubt that people ever lived on Mars.

2 Complete the conversation with the sentences from Exercise 1.

Josh: Look at this article, Brian. It says that at one time there might have been life on Mars. Do you believe that's possible?

Brian: Well, <u>I doubt that people ever lived on Mars</u>¹. I mean, scientists would have figured that out.

Josh: I agree that people couldn't have lived on Mars. _____² _____.

Brian: What do you mean?

Josh: Well, you know, like plant life. _____³.

Brian: No way! _____⁴. Scientists . . .

Josh: OK, OK. Maybe you're right. _____⁵. I think there are rivers or maybe even a lake.

Brian: Well, *maybe* in the past, but I don't think there's that much water now. . . . Hey, would you go to Mars if you had the chance?

Josh: _____⁶. But if I did get the chance, I guess I would go!

68   Unit 9   Lesson B

C History's mysteries

1 Complete the news report with the words from the box.

abduction	discovery	explosion
✓ disappearance	escape	theft

"Coming up tonight on PSB news in Miami . . . Our first story, from Houston, Texas, is about the ____disappearance____ (1) of Terrance Wellington, a well-known Houston artist. His family says they haven't seen him since Tuesday morning. Next, Jamie Sanders is in Mexico, and she'll tell you about the _____ (2) of a new pyramid near Mexico City. That's exciting news because a new pyramid has not been found in several years. In San Francisco, we have news about a big _____ (3). People in the area say the noise was frightening and extremely loud. Two restaurants burned. And don't miss this story . . . There was a _____ (4) in a museum in New York on Saturday. Robbers took a painting worth 15 million dollars. We also have a local story that happened right here in Florida. Carl Frey will tell you about a prison _____ (5). Two men broke out of a prison in Jacksonville. Fortunately, police caught them a few hours later. And our last story tonight is about an alien _____ (6). Is it true or not? Dan Alvarado interviews two people in Phoenix, Arizona, who claim they were taken aboard a UFO by aliens. All this and more after these messages."

2 Label each picture with the number and word from the correct news story in Exercise 1.

_____ _____

_____ _____

(prison tower image)
_____ _____

_____ _____

(MISSING man image)
__1__ __disappearance__

_____ _____

3 Circle the correct words to complete the conversation.

Greg: Hi, Ahn. Do you have any idea **(what)** / **if** a total solar eclipse is?

Ahn: Sure. It's what happens when the moon is between the sun and earth.

Greg: Oh, OK. Do you know **how** / **if** that's why the sky gets black?

Ahn: Yes, it is. You can't see light from the sun because of where the moon is.

Greg: And can you tell me **how long** / **what** it lasts?

Ahn: Well, it depends. The shortest eclipses are usually about a minute.

Greg: Do you have any idea **how long** / **how many** the longest eclipse can be?

Ahn: It can be over seven minutes, but that hardly ever happens.

Greg: Do you know **how tall** / **if** solar eclipses happen every year?

Ahn: Yes, they do.

Greg: And can you tell me **how many** / **if** there are each year?

Ahn: There can be between two and five eclipses each year, but there can never be more than two total eclipses.

Greg: Interesting. Thanks, Ahn.

4 Write embedded yes / no questions with the words in parentheses. Use the simple past.

1. (Can you tell me / Zorro / be / a real person)
   <u>Can you tell me if Zorro was a real person?</u>

2. (Do you know / anyone / find / Amelia Earhart's plane)
   _____

3. (Do you have any idea / the Egyptians / build / the first pyramid)
   _____

4. (Can you tell me / people / find / an underwater pyramid in Japan)
   _____

5. (Do you have any idea / anyone / escape / from Alcatraz prison)
   _____

6. (Do you know / the abduction / be / on the news)
   _____

5 Look at B's responses. Use *Can you tell me* or *Do you know* to write embedded *Wh-* questions about these famous places.

1. **A:** <u>Can you tell me how long the Tsing Ma Bridge is?</u>

   B: Yes, I can. The Tsing Ma Bridge is about 1.4 kilometers long.

2. **A:** <u>Do you know   ?</u>

   B: Yes, I do. The Eiffel Tower is 324 meters tall.

3. **A:** _____

   B: Yes, I can. Two people escaped from Alcatraz prison.

4. **A:** _____

   B: Yes, I can. The Sphinx is 60 meters long.

5. **A:** _____

   B: Yes, I do. The Pyramid of the Sun is about 75 meters tall.

6. **A:** _____

   B: Yes, I do. There are about 13,000 taxis in New York City.

6 Answer the questions with *Yes* or *No*. Add more information.

Example: <u>No. But I know there are over one million.</u>   or
            <u>Yes, There are 2.5 million people in my country.</u>

1. Do you know how many people there are in your country?
   _____

2. Do you have any idea what the population of your city is?
   _____

3. Do you know if there are any mysteries about people or places in your country?
   _____

4. Do you have any idea what famous writers are from your country?
   _____

5. Do you know where famous people go for vacation in your country?
   _____

D Explanations from long ago

1 Read the magazine interview. What is rongorongo? Circle the correct answer.

a. the name of a people   b. the name of a writing system   c. the name of an island

Lisa Olsen talks about rongorongo with Dr. Gomez . . .

EASTER ISLAND, in the Pacific Ocean, is famous for its large stone statues that were made hundreds of years ago. But not many people know about rongorongo. It is the name of the writing found on tablets, large pieces of wood, on Easter Island. I spoke with Dr. Ramiro Gomez about this mysterious writing system.

Q: Dr. Gomez, what is rongorongo?

A: Rongorongo is a writing system found on Easter Island. It doesn't have letters like English. It uses *glyphs*, which are pictures or symbols, to represent different things. In the 1860s, people discovered wooden tablets with the rongorongo glyphs on them. Today, there are only 21 of these tablets. The rest have disappeared.

Q: Can you tell me what the tablets say?

A: Many people have tried to figure out what the different glyphs mean. But so far, no one has figured out rongorongo completely. Some of the glyphs look like different animals in the area . . . birds, sea turtles, and fish. It also seems that some of the glyphs represent plants. We're pretty sure that one of the tablets has a calendar on it, but no one has figured out exactly how the calendar works.

Q: Do you know how and when the tablets were made?

A: We know that the glyphs were carved with shark's teeth. We also know that they are very old. Researchers say they might have been made in the late 1600s.

Q: If we can't read the language, are the tablets useless?

A: Definitely not. They still tell us a lot about the people who made them. For example, they had their own written language and wanted to record their history.

Q: Is there more to learn from the tablets?

A: Yes, there is. People will be studying rongorongo for many years. Hopefully, someone will solve the mystery of what is on the tablets.

2 Read the interview again. Write T (true), F (false), or NI (no information).

1. Rongorongo has 21 letters. __F__
2. Some of the symbols in rongorongo look like animals. _____
3. There are sea turtles near Easter Island. _____
4. The symbols were made with shark's teeth. _____
5. Rongorongo doesn't tell us anything. _____
6. Dr. Gomez will continue researching rongorongo. _____

Perspectives

A A traffic accident

1 Put the words in the correct order to make sentences.

1. Brenda / care / her sister's cat / takes / on weekends / of / .

   <u>Brenda takes care of her sister's cat</u>
   <u>on weekends.</u>

2. with / up / comes / great ideas / Larry / .

   _____

3. doesn't put / send text messages in class / students / Ms. Nelson / up / with / who / .

   _____

4. friends / with / up / on the Internet / catches / Paulina / .

   _____

5. going through / shouldn't get / Drivers / away with / a red light / .

   _____

6. looks / to / Arturo / his favorite musician / up / .

   _____

7. along / all of his classmates / gets / Omar / with / .

   _____

8. to their trip / forward / Sandra and Mike / are looking / to Peru / .

   _____

2 Write sentences with your own information.

Example: <u>I get along with my sister and my friend Josh.</u>

1. Two people you get along with: _____
2. Two characteristics you can't put up with: _____
3. One person you look up to: _____
4. Two things you're looking forward to: _____

Unit 10 Lesson A 73

3 Circle the correct verb form to complete each sentence.

1. **Kendra:** "I saw an accident on Main Street."

   Kendra said that she _____ an accident on Main Street.

   a. sees   b. has seen   (c.) had seen

2. **Jack:** "I look up to my grandfather."

   Jack told me he _____ to his grandfather.

   a. will look up   b. looked up   c. would look up

3. **Shan:** "I will take care of my brother's daughter."

   Shan said she _____ of her brother's daughter.

   a. would take care   b. won't take care   c. is taking care

4. **Sibel:** "The driver of the car has disappeared!"

   Sibel told me that the driver of the car _____ .

   a. had disappeared   b. were disappearing   c. disappear

5. **Matt:** "I'm getting along well with my roommates."

   Matt told me that he _____ with his roommates.

   a. has gotten along well   b. was getting along well   c. would get along well

6. **Ricardo:** "I have a doctor's appointment."

   Ricardo said he _____ a doctor's appointment.

   a. has had   b. had had   c. had

4 Match each sentence to the correct picture.

1. She said that she was working on Tuesday.
2. She said that she had worked on Tuesday.
3. She said that she worked on Tuesday.
4. She said that she would work on Tuesday.

"I work on Tuesday."

"I am working on Tuesday."

"I worked on Tuesday."

"I will work on Tuesday."

5 Complete the sentences. Use *said* or *told* and reported speech. Use *that* if you wish.

1. **Olivia:** "I have an important meeting, Doug."
   Olivia _____told_____ Doug _(that) she had an important meeting_____ .

2. **John:** "I did well on my test."
   John _____ .

3. **Paula:** "I'm riding my bicycle to the movie theater, Sue."
   Paula _____ Sue _____ .

4. **Victor:** "I'll tell the police about the accident."
   Victor _____ me _____ .

5. **Fred:** "I have come up with a great idea for your birthday."
   Fred _____ .

6. **Sally:** "A UFO is sitting in front of my house."
   Sally _____ .

6 Read the news story. Then write what each person said.

ROBBER ESCAPES WITH EXPENSIVE PAINTING

Last night there was a theft at the art museum. The museum director said, "A robber has taken a painting worth $2 million." Many people were visiting the museum at the time. Oliver Jones, 52, told a police officer, "I saw a man leave the museum with a large bag." Cindy Milton, 33, was there with her two sons but could offer no help. "I didn't see anything," she said. The theft is surprising because the museum is in a quiet, safe neighborhood. Jen Kennedy, a 25-year-old art student, told reporters, "I am surprised and a little scared." Tom Weston, 76, said, "The robber won't get away with it!" Donna Lawrence, who works at the museum, agrees with Weston. She told reporters, "The police are already looking for the robber." Then she said, "He will get caught." If you saw anything that might help catch the robber, please call the police.

1. The museum director _said that a robber had taken a painting worth $2 million_ .
2. Oliver Jones _told a police officer that_ _____ .
3. Cindy Milton _____ .
4. Jen Kennedy _____ .
5. Tom Weston _____ .
6. Donna Lawrence _____ .
7. Then she _____ .

B As I was saying, . . .

Complete the conversations with the sentences from the box.

> To get back to what I was saying, I'm really upset with Melanie.
> By the way, I saw a great movie on Friday.
> I just thought of something.
> ✓ That reminds me, I chatted with Ellie online last night.
> To finish what I was saying, I'm going on vacation next week.
> But as I was saying, the Internet is a great way to connect with old friends.

A. **Ana:** I love catching up with friends online.

  Lei: <u>That reminds me, I chatted with Ellie</u>
   <u>online last night.</u>
   We talked for an hour!

  Ana: Really? How is she doing?

  Lei: She's great. She told me she had moved to Canada.

  Ana: Wow. That's interesting. _____2

  Lei: It really is. I wonder if my old friend Blanca ever chats online.

  Ana: I bet you could find her by using one of those websites for finding old friends.

B. **Sarah:** You know, I can't put up with people who lie.

  Drew: Who lied to you?

  Sarah: Well, Melanie told me she couldn't go the movies with me because she was sick, but then Tom told me they went to the movie together.

  Drew: _____1

  Sarah: What did you see?

  Drew: That new Brad Pitt movie.

  Sarah: That sounds great. _____2

C. **Carl:** Martin is taking care of my plants while I'm on vacation.

  Tito: Hey, _____1

  Carl: What?

  Tito: I heard that Joe's Green Place is having a sale on plants. Do you want to go?

  Carl: Sure. We could go tomorrow. _____2

C There's always an explanation.

1 Complete the puzzle and the sentences with the correct verbs.

Across

1. I don't _____ on going to the restaurant with you tonight. It's too expensive.
4. We can't _____ on a dress. Do you like the blue one or the red one?
6. I don't _____ in UFOs, but my brother thinks they are real.
7. I never _____ about my problems. It always seems to be OK in the end.
8. You can _____ on me. I'll help you with anything.

Down

1. Carmela doesn't _____ in many sports, but she plays tennis with her family.
2. Don't _____ about your mother. You have to pick her up at the airport today.
3. Nick can _____ on his sister. She is always helpful when he needs her.
4. I didn't _____ about anything while I was sleeping last night.
5. Did you _____ about Brendon? John said that he was going to Spain!

2 Answer the questions with your own information.

Example: _I worry about my classes._ or _I worry about my children._

1. What or who do you worry about? _____
2. What sports do you participate in? _____
3. Who can you depend on? _____
4. What do you plan on doing this weekend? _____
5. What have you dreamed about more than once? _____

3 Read about Brianna and Rafael's conversation. Then write T (true) or F (false).

> Brianna asked Rafael if he was OK. Rafael said he was fine. Then Rafael asked Brianna if she had gone to the Wakes concert last night. Brianna told him that she hadn't gone. Rafael said that he had gone to the concert and it had been great. Brianna said she was sorry she hadn't gone. Then she asked if the Wakes were playing again soon. Rafael told her that they were. He said they would play at the CC Café on Friday. Brianna said that she would definitely go on Friday. Then she said she was looking forward to it.

1. Brianna wanted to know how Rafael was. __T__
2. Brianna went to the concert last night. _____
3. Rafael went to the concert last night. _____
4. Rafael thought the concert was bad. _____
5. The Wakes aren't playing on Friday. _____
6. Brianna is planning to go to the next concert. _____

4 Circle the correct verb form to complete the reported speech in each sentence.

1. **Jim:** "Hey, Dina, do you plan on going to Doug's party?"

   Jim asked Dina if she **is planning** / **(planned)** on going to Doug's party.

2. **Larissa:** "Did you hear about the big storm, Kayla?"

   Larissa asked Kayla if she **had heard** / **was hearing** about the big storm.

3. **Nancy:** "Will you take care of my cat next week, Janet?"

   Nancy asked Janet if she **would take care of** / **took care of** her cat next week.

4. **Jason:** "Are you driving to Chicago, Tiago?"

   Jason asked Tiago if he **drives** / **was driving** to Chicago.

5. **Linda:** "Hey, Tim, have you tried the dumplings yet?"

   Linda asked Tim if he **would try** / **had tried** the dumplings yet.

6. **Sakura:** "Are you nervous about the test, Dan?"

   Sakura asked Dan if he **is** / **was** nervous about the test.

7. **Mario:** "Hi, Lori. Do you want to go shopping?"

   Mario asked Lori if she **wanted** / **had wanted** to go shopping.

5 Complete the sentences with the correct pronouns.

1. **Jennifer:** "Mom, are you tired?"

   Jennifer asked her mother if ___she___ was tired.

2. **Carol:** "Joe, have you seen my sister?"

   Carol asked Joe if _____ had seen _____ sister.

3. **Jack:** "Will you help me with my homework?"

   Jack asked me if I would help _____ with _____ homework.

4. **Debbie:** "Hi, Mr. and Mrs. Lee. Are you going to buy a new car?"

   Debbie asked Mr. and Mrs. Lee if _____ were going to buy a new car.

5. **Mr. Garza:** "Good morning, students. Have you done your homework?"

   Mr. Garza asked the students if _____ had done _____ homework.

6 Read the conversation. Then rewrite the underlined questions as reported questions.

Erica: I'm really worried.

Paul: <u>Are you worried about Ben?</u> He wasn't in class yesterday.

Erica: Yes, I am. <u>Have you talked to him?</u>

Paul: No, I haven't, but I'm sure he's OK.

Erica: <u>Will you call him?</u>

Paul: I guess so. Why? <u>Is your phone at home?</u>

Erica: No, but I don't want to call him. I'm embarrassed.

Paul: Embarrassed? What's going on? <u>Did you and Ben have a fight?</u>

Erica: Oh, no. I had a dream about him last night. He was in an accident in the dream, and now I want to make sure he's OK.

Paul: OK. I'll call him. <u>Do you have Ben's number?</u>

Erica: It's 820-555-2962. <u>Are you going to tell Ben about my dream?</u> Please don't!

1. Paul asked Erica ___if she was worried about Ben___.
2. Erica asked Paul _____.
3. Erica asked Paul _____.
4. Paul asked Erica _____.
5. Paul asked Erica _____.
6. Paul asked Erica _____.
7. Erica asked Paul _____.

Unit 10 Lesson C 79

D Thoughts, values, and experiences

1 Read the story. Who is in the audience during the TV show?

_____

Inside the Actor's Studio

James Lipton is a TV host in the United States. He has a TV show called *Inside the Actor's Studio* that has been on TV since 1994. He interviews actors and actresses about their careers. He's also a teacher at a university. The audience is always students from his acting classes. The hour-long interviews are always interesting, but people really look forward to the end of the show. At the end, Lipton asks his guests questions based on the Proust Questionnaire. He asks each guest the same ten questions every week. Some of the questions are: *What's your favorite word?*, *What's your least favorite word?*, *What sound or noise do you love?*, and *What sound or noise do you hate?*

Many actors have given similar answers to the questions. When actress Gwyneth Paltrow was on the show, Lipton asked her what sound or noise she loved. She said that she loved the sound of her mother's voice when she said "goodnight." When Johnny Depp answered the same question, he said that he loved the sound of his daughter's voice. Angelina Jolie said she loved the sound of her son when he couldn't stop laughing. Jolie said her least favorite sound was children in pain. Comedian and actor Dave Chappelle said he didn't like the sound of children crying.

Depp told Lipton that his favorite word was *why* and his least favorite word was *no*. Chappelle, Jolie, and actor Will Smith also said their least favorite word was *no*. Jolie said her favorite word was *now*.

Lipton has also heard some interesting and unique answers to the questionnaire over the years. Singer Jennifer Lopez said her favorite word was *love* and her least favorite word was *can't*. British actor Hugh Laurie said that his favorite word was *marsupial*, which is a word that describes animals with a pouch, like a kangaroo. Several of Laurie's answers were funny. He said his favorite noise was someone playing a guitar badly. Lipton asked him why, and Laurie said he couldn't explain it.

After the questions are finished, Lipton's students get to come up with their own questions to ask the guest. Lipton wants to entertain his audience, but he believes in giving his acting students an interesting way to learn.

2 Read the story again. Then write T (true), F (false), or NI (no information).

1. Before *Inside the Actor's Studio*, James Lipton used to be an actor. __NI__
2. Lipton asks all guests the same questions based on the Proust Questionnaire. _____
3. Johnny Depp has a son, but he doesn't have a daughter. _____
4. Many of the guests mentioned in the story said their favorite word was *yes*. _____
5. Hugh Laurie's favorite word is *kangaroo*. _____
6. Lipton's students ask the guests interesting questions. _____

The real world

A Getting it done

1 Complete the text with the correct phrases from the box.

accepted the job offer	printed the email	researched the job
applied for the job	✓ proofread and formatted his résumé	sent a thank-you note
prepare for the interview	provide references	translate a letter

John Torres didn't have a job after he finished college, but he worked hard to find one. First, he wrote his résumé. His friend Kyle __proofread and formatted his résumé__ for him. John had forgotten to _____(2)_____ on his résumé, so Kyle added them. John looked for jobs on the Internet. He saw an ad for a translator, and he _____(3)_____ . Mrs. Baker from TB Trans called him to schedule an interview. Kyle helped him _____(4)_____ . He asked John questions that he thought Mrs. Baker would ask. John _____(5)_____ , and he read a lot of information about the company. Before the interview, he _____(6)_____ from Mrs. Baker with the directions to her office. His interview went really well. He went home and _____(7)_____ to Mrs. Baker. Two days later, Mrs. Baker offered him a job. John _____(8)_____ . His first assignment was to _____(9)_____ from English to Spanish.

2 Answer the questions with your own information.

Example: _Yes, I have. I looked up information about the company online, and I practiced answering questions._

1. Have you ever had a job interview? What did you do to prepare for it?

   _____

2. Have you ever made a résumé? Who proofread it?

   _____

3. Have you ever accepted a job offer? What job was it?

   _____

Unit 11 Lesson A 81

3 Read each sentence. Then check (✓) the correct answer to the question.

1. John gets Pete to print the business cards.
   Who prints the business cards? ☐ John ✓ Pete

2. Martha has her clothes washed at Mindy's Laundry.
   Does Martha wash her own clothes? ☐ Yes ☐ No

3. Yoko had her reference letter translated.
   Did someone translate Yoko's reference letter? ☐ Yes ☐ No

4. Mr. Clark gets Ned to photocopy his important papers.
   Who photocopies the papers? ☐ Mr. Clark ☐ Ned

5. Frank has Ben wash his car on the weekends.
   Who washes the car? ☐ Frank ☐ Ben

6. Jennifer plans to get her hair cut on Tuesday.
   Will Jennifer cut her own hair? ☐ Yes ☐ No

4 Complete the text with the correct phrases from the box.

get a friend to help you	have someone clean
get a neighbor to take care of	have your bank pay
get your clothes washed	✓ have your clothes dry-cleaned

Create More Time at Home

- Are you tired of doing laundry? Do you have nice suits and dresses? _Have your clothes dry-cleaned_ (1). You can also _____ (2) at many places.

- Don't stress about a clean house. _____ (3) your house for you. It's a little expensive, but it will give you time for other things.

- If you have children, get some help. _____ (4) your children for a few hours. Then you can get things done.

- _____ (5) with jobs around the house. Later, you can help your friend. It is sometimes more fun to work together.

- Set up automatic payments and _____ (6) your bills automatically. It's easy and saves you time. You don't have to worry about late bills.

5 Circle the correct word to complete each sentence.

1. Rachel (has)/ gets her sister translate letters for her.
2. Sammy **has** / **gets** Jeff to do the laundry.
3. Mario and Camila **have** / **get** FoTake print their photos.
4. I usually **have** / **get** my father to drive me to the airport.
5. Asami **has** / **gets** Jessie to help her with her homework.
6. We **have** / **get** Park Press print our business cards.
7. Do you **have** / **get** anyone proofread your résumé?
8. Who do you **get** / **have** to clean your house?
9. Josh **has** / **gets** Pam feed his cat when he's on vacation.
10. Mona **has** / **gets** her neighbor to pick up her mail when she's in London.

6 Look at Michio's "To Do" list. He has checked (✓) the things that he has already gotten done. Write sentences about what he has already had done and what he still needs to have done. Use the verbs in parentheses.

TO DO
1. suits – dry-clean ✓
2. shirts – iron
3. hair – cut ✓
4. apartment – clean
5. résumé – proofread ✓
6. résumé – translate into English
7. business cards – print ✓
8. car – fix

1. (have) *Michio had his suits dry-cleaned.*
2. (get)   *He needs to get his shirts ironed.*
3. (get)   _____
4. (have) _____
5. (get)   _____
6. (have) _____
7. (have) _____
8. (get)   _____

B Let me see . . .

1 Three people are interviewing for a job as a salesperson. Complete the interviews with sentences from the box. Sometimes more than one answer is possible. Use each sentence only once.

Hmm, let me think.	Well, it's been great talking to you.
✓ Oh . . . let's see.	Well, it's been nice meeting you.
Um, let me see.	Well, I've really enjoyed talking to you.

A. Interviewer: One more question, Ms. Jones. What is your greatest strength?

   Ms. Jones: Well, I really enjoy working with people.

   Interviewer: OK. And what do you like best about working with people?

   Ms. Jones: <u>Oh . . . let's see.</u>
   ₁
   I like to learn new things from them. I also like to help other people get things done.

   Interviewer: Very good. _____
   ₂
   We'll call you in a few days.

B. Interviewer: I have one last question, Mr. Harris. What is your greatest strength?

   Mr. Harris: _____
   ₁
   I know . . . I'm very outgoing. I love to talk to people.

   Interviewer: _____
   ₂

   Mr. Harris: Thanks. Did I get the job?

   Interviewer: We have a few more interviews. We'll call you in a few days.

C. Interviewer: OK, I have only one more question. What is your greatest strength?

   Mr. Gomez: I'm very responsible. I'm always on time. I'm also energetic and hardworking. Oh, and I'm very good with computers.

   Interviewer: OK. And if you had to pick one thing . . . which one would it be?

   Mr. Gomez: _____ I guess that I'm
   ₁
   responsible. I think it's important to be on time and to get your work done.

   Interviewer: _____ Thank you
   ₂
   for coming in for this interview, Mr. Gomez. We'll call you in a few days.

2 Who do you think would be best for the job? Check (✓) your answer.

☐ Ms. Jones   ☐ Mr. Harris   ☐ Mr. Gomez

C Future goals

1 Complete the text with the correct phrases from the box.

- doing volunteer work
- having a big wedding
- live in the countryside
- ✓ 'm already financially independent
- 'm working as a journalist
- preparing for my exams
- studying abroad
- write travel books

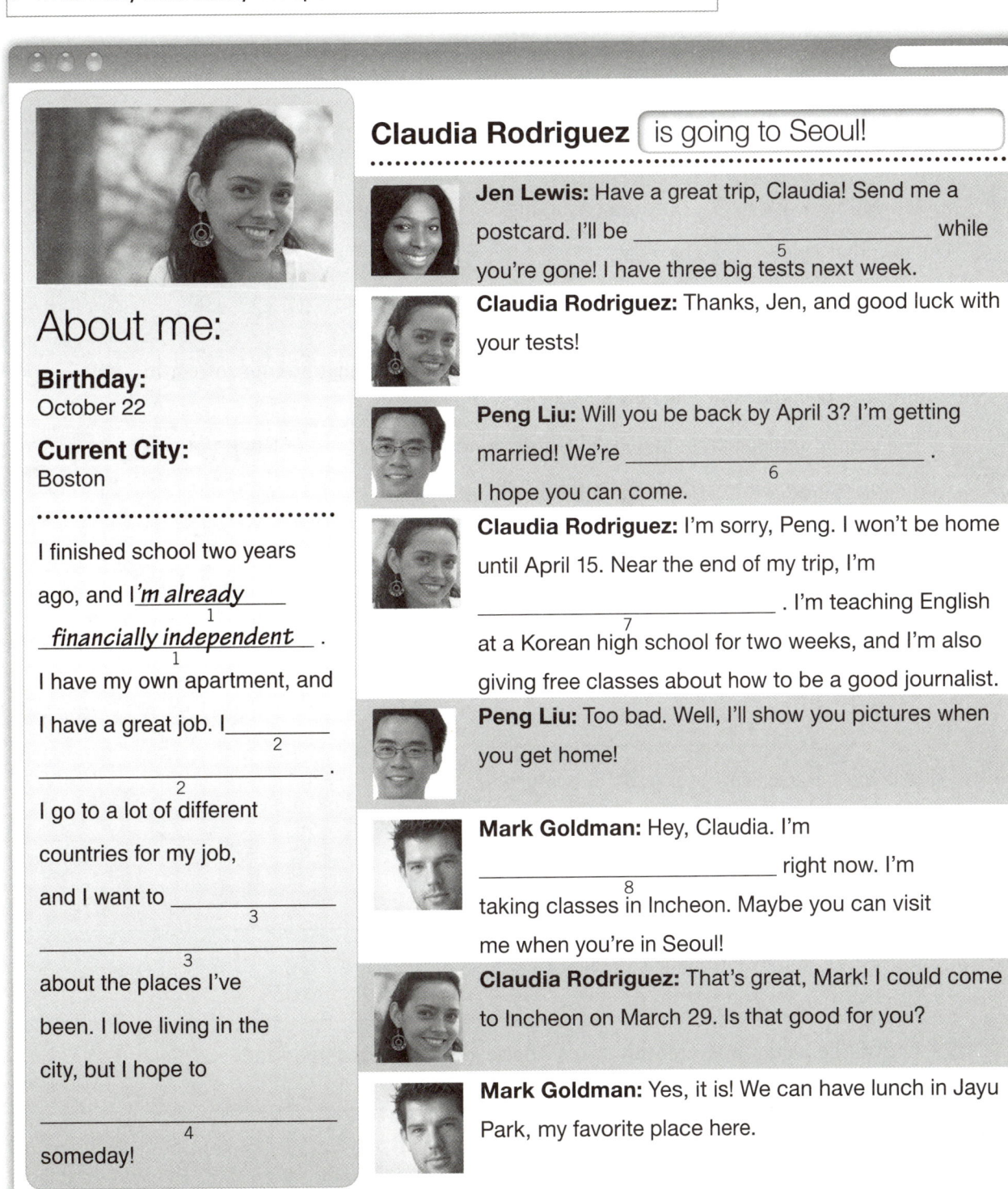

Claudia Rodriguez is going to Seoul!

About me:

Birthday:
October 22

Current City:
Boston

I finished school two years ago, and I _'m already financially independent_ ¹. I have my own apartment, and I have a great job. I _____² _____². I go to a lot of different countries for my job, and I want to _____³ _____³ about the places I've been. I love living in the city, but I hope to _____⁴ someday!

Jen Lewis: Have a great trip, Claudia! Send me a postcard. I'll be _____⁵ while you're gone! I have three big tests next week.

Claudia Rodriguez: Thanks, Jen, and good luck with your tests!

Peng Liu: Will you be back by April 3? I'm getting married! We're _____⁶. I hope you can come.

Claudia Rodriguez: I'm sorry, Peng. I won't be home until April 15. Near the end of my trip, I'm _____⁷. I'm teaching English at a Korean high school for two weeks, and I'm also giving free classes about how to be a good journalist.

Peng Liu: Too bad. Well, I'll show you pictures when you get home!

Mark Goldman: Hey, Claudia. I'm _____⁸ right now. I'm taking classes in Incheon. Maybe you can visit me when you're in Seoul!

Claudia Rodriguez: That's great, Mark! I could come to Incheon on March 29. Is that good for you?

Mark Goldman: Yes, it is! We can have lunch in Jayu Park, my favorite place here.

2 Circle the correct verb form to complete each sentence.

1. What _____ next year?
   a. will you be   b. were you doing   (c.) will you be doing

2. Jacob _____ Chinese at a university next year.
   a. will be studying   b. be studying   c. was studying

3. Tonya _____ her new car by next week.
   a. having   b. will be having   c. will have

4. Larry and Samantha _____ financially independent in a year.
   a. were being   b. will be   c. will be being

5. _____ with Mr. Harding this week?
   a. Will you be working   b. You are working   c. Working

6. I'm sure that Kyle _____ his goals.
   a. will be achieving   b. will achieve   c. achieving

3 Check (✓) the sentences that are correct. Change the sentences that are not correct to the future with *will* and write the new sentence.

1. ☐ Will you be remembering my birthday in two months?
   Will you remember my birthday in two months?

2. ☐ Min Woo will be preparing for his exams this weekend.
   _____

3. ☐ Susana will be being financially independent when she gets a job.
   _____

4. ☐ Will you be achieving your goals in two years?
   _____

5. ☐ Beatriz will be doing volunteer work on Saturday.
   _____

6. ☐ Do you think they'll be having a good time in Spain?
   _____

7. ☐ Tim will be working as a doctor in Los Angeles for the next three years.
   _____

8. ☐ We'll be believing your story when you prove it.
   _____

4 Complete the email with the future continuous of the verbs in parentheses.

Hi Fatih!

How are you? Will you be home soon? We miss you in class. This week we had to write about what we think our lives will be like in the future. I started thinking about it a lot. Five years from now, I <u>won't be working</u> (not / work)¹ for a large company. Instead, I _____² (work) as a travel writer. I _____³ (live) in a large apartment in the city. I _____⁴ (travel) a lot for work. I _____⁵ (go) to Mexico and Brazil. I don't know if all this will happen, but it's OK to dream, right?

What do you think you _____⁶ (do) in five years? _____⁷ you _____⁷ (study) abroad?

Your friend,
Nick

5 Complete the email with the future with *will* of the verbs in parentheses.

Hey Nick!

It was great to hear from you. I <u>'ll be</u>¹ (be) home on Tuesday. I'm having a great time in Spain. Your question was interesting. Let's see . . . in five years, what will I be doing? Well, first I _____² (finish) school next year, but then I _____³ (go) to work for my father. In five years, I _____⁴ (not / be) his assistant. I _____⁵ (have) to make the decisions! I hope I _____⁶ (meet) someone really nice in the next few years, but I _____⁷ (not / be) married in five years. I do think that I'll be living in the countryside. _____⁸ you _____⁸ (visit) me there?

See you soon!
Fatih

6 What will you be doing in five years? Write two sentences about each topic.

Example: <u>I'll be studying abroad in Canada. Maybe I'll learn French!</u>

1. School: _____

2. Work: _____

3. Travel: _____

Unit 11 Lesson C 87

D My career

1 Read the article. What is causing some jobs to disappear?

DISAPPEARING JOBS

Have you ever thought about jobs disappearing? As technology improves and new things are invented, some jobs are no longer needed. For example, before the invention of the automatic elevator, there were elevator operators. The operator controlled the elevator as it went up and down, and he or she opened and closed the doors of the elevator. Once elevators became automated, this job was no longer needed. Here are some other jobs that might disappear some day.

Travel Agents: In the past, people had travel agents plan their trips and buy their tickets. Today, it is easy to buy plane tickets online. It's also easy to research different places to go, find hotels, rent cars, and much more. There will be fewer travel agents in the future because more and more people will be planning their vacations online.

Bank Tellers: Bank tellers inside a bank help you get cash, deposit your checks, and transfer money. But since the invention of automated teller machines (ATMs), online banking, and banking by phone, many people rarely go inside a bank. They don't need to get help from the bank teller because they can use new technologies to do those things at the ATM, online, or by phone.

Photo Processors: Photo processors develop and print pictures. With the invention of digital cameras, the need for this job has been reduced. Many stores now have machines that print digital pictures. Even these types of stores are disappearing because many people now print their pictures at home.

Video Store Clerks: People don't have to go to video stores to rent movies anymore. They can rent them from companies that send movies in the mail. Many videos can also be streamed online. It's possible that there won't be any video stores in the future.

We'll know in time which of these jobs will last and which ones won't. We'll also see what other jobs might disappear as technology improves. Even though some jobs are lost, technology also creates new jobs. For example, someone has to put money in ATM machines and repair them when they break.

2 Read the article again. Write T (true), F (false), or NI (no information).

1. The automatic elevator was invented 100 years ago. __NI__
2. There are no travel agents now. _____
3. Because of ATMs, people never go into banks now. _____
4. A lot of people print photographs at home. _____
5. It's very expensive to stream videos online. _____
6. New jobs are often created when old ones disappear. _____

unit 12

Finding solutions

A Environmental concerns

1 Complete the sentences and the puzzle with the correct verbs. What's the mystery word?

1. Dana wants to _____ her old computer, but she doesn't know where to take it.
2. Lydia _____ tasks when she goes out in her car. For example, she buys food at a store near her office.
3. Don't _____ oil on the ground.
4. Jack's car is in great condition. He _____ it by checking the oil often.
5. You should _____ where the recycling room is in your new apartment building.

¹R E C Y C L E

2 Complete the text with the correct verbs from the box.

avoid	conserve	limit	store
commute	discard	purchase	✓recycle

Simple Ways You Can Reduce Pollution

- ___Recycle___₁ items like newspapers, magazines, and plastic bottles from your home.

- _____₂ products that are harmful for the environment. Instead, _____₃ "green" products for your home.

- _____₄ old batteries and printer ink properly. Be sure you _____₅ them in a safe place until you find the right place to throw them away.

- How do you _____₆ to work? Can you walk, take a bus, or ride a bicycle to work? If you have to drive, try to go to work with other people in your car.

- _____₇ water. When you wash your hair or brush your teeth, turn the water off until you are ready to use it again. In this way, you can _____₈ how much water you use.

Unit 12 Lesson A 89

3 Complete the sentences with the present continuous passive of the verb in parentheses.

STAYING GREEN

Many hotels do things that are not good for the environment. For example, water _is being wasted_ (waste) every day in many hotels, and many items _____ (not / recycle). The good news is that there is a growing number of "green" hotels around the world. The Alto Hotel in Melbourne, Australia, is one that is making a difference. For example, the lights at the hotel are powered by wind energy, and the guests' newspapers are recycled every day. Other environmentally friendly things _____ (do) every day at the Alto Hotel, too. If you go there, you'll see that "green" cleaning products _____ (use) to clean the rooms. Rain water _____ (collect and store) at the hotel and then used later for cleaning and for watering plants. Hotel guests _____ (teach) how to help the environment, too. The hotel gives people free parking if they drive electric or hybrid cars. And guests _____ (remind) that they can walk to places close to the hotel. Not only is the hotel environmentally friendly, it's a beautiful place to stay, too.

4 Write sentences with the verbs in parentheses. Use the simple present with the infinitive passive.

1. (Something / have / do / about the parking problem)
   Something has to be done about the parking problem.

2. (More "green" buildings / need / create)
   _____

3. (Chemicals / have / store / in safe containers)
   _____

4. (Batteries / have / discard / properly)
   _____

5. (More water / need / conserve)
   _____

6. (Newspapers / need / recycle)
   _____

5 Circle the correct words to complete the conversation.

Rosa: Something has **(to be done)** / **is being done** about the pollution in this city.

Jake: I agree that the problem needs **to be taken care of** / **is being taken care of**, but it's too big for us to do anything about it.

Rosa: We can help a lot! A lot of pollution **to be made** / **is being made** by our cars.

Jake: But we have to get to work!

Rosa: There are other ways to go. You know, in some cities cars **not to be allowed** / **aren't being allowed** on the road with only one person.

Jake: Hmm, that's interesting. I guess if changes have **to be made** / **are being made**, people will make them!

Rosa: Maybe we can talk to people at work and start a carpool . . . you know, ride together.

Jake: That's a good idea. That new highway **to be built** / **is being built** right now. It will be easy for me to pick up you and Tonya on my way to work.

Rosa: That'd be great. But don't remind me about the new highway! Think of all the pollution that **to be created** / **is being created** by all those cars!

6 Complete the sentences with your own ideas about your country. If you need help, you can use some of the words in the box.

clean	fix	paper	pollution	technology
conserve	health clinics	parks	recycle	trash
education	newspapers	plastic	recycling programs	waste

Example: _Something has to be done about maintaining our bridges._ or

Something has to be done about the pollution in our air.

1. Something has to be done about _____ .
2. Not enough money is being spent on _____ .
3. A lot of money is being spent on _____ .
4. _____ is / are being recycled.
5. _____ isn't / aren't being recycled.
6. The highways need to be _____ .

Unit 12   Lesson A   91

B That's a good point.

1 Complete the conversation with the sentences from the box.

> I see it a little differently.
> It's better to pay more for something that doesn't harm the environment.
> Thanks. I like the idea of "green" products.
> That's great, but these products are really expensive.
> ✓This store is great. They only sell "green" products.
> Wow. You make a very good point.
> Yes, but you have the money to pay more.

Ken: <u>This store is great. They only sell "green" products.</u>

Bill: _____

Ken: I think that's OK. _____

Bill: _____

I think everyone should be able to buy products that help the environment.

Ken: Well, I don't mind paying more!

Bill: _____

What about people who don't have the money? They should be able to buy "green" products, too.

Ken: _____

Bill: _____

I just think they should be cheaper.

2 What do you think about these opinions? Use a phrase from the box to give your own response.

> Actually, I have a different opinion.   I see what you mean.
> I don't see it that way.   That's a good point.

1. **Ken:** People should have to drive with two or more people in their cars.

   You: _____

2. **Bill:** People shouldn't have to recycle if they don't want to.

   You: _____

C My community

1 Label each picture with the correct community improvement phrase. Use one word from each box.

✓ beautification	employment	neighborhood	recreation
community	health	public	recycling

center	center	garden	✓ project
center	clinic	library	watch

1. _beautification project_
2. _____
3. _____
4. _____
5. _____
6. _____
7. _____
8. _____

Unit 12   Lesson C   93

2 Put the words in the correct order to make sentences.

1. don't recycle / a recycling center here, / Although / there's / many people / .

   Although there's a recycling center here, many people don't recycle.

2. after school / Jen goes / Jen's mom / so / works late, / to a recreation center / .

   _____

3. a city rule / because of / We / about maintaining cars / have cleaner air / .

   _____

4. a beautification project / so that / this area / We / will look better / should start / .

   _____

5. Our yard / at the garden center / we / if / will look nice / get plants / .

   _____

3 Circle the correct words to complete the email.

Dear Councilman Sunders:

I am a concerned citizen in your area. **So** / **(Although)** the city council office is working to fight crime in our neighborhood, we still need more help. This is a significant problem, and many people in the neighborhood no longer go out at night **if** / **because of** the crime. A few of my neighbors and I want to try to help solve the problem. We feel things will get better **if** / **so** we start a neighborhood watch. But we don't think that's enough. We think the police need to be in our neighborhood more **because of** / **so** criminals know they will get caught. We're dedicated to changing things, **so** / **although** we will be at the next community meeting on May 8 at 7:00 p.m. in the Oakmont Community Center. We hope you or someone from your office will be there **because of** / **so that** you can help. **Although** / **If** this email may seem negative, we appreciate your work on the city council. I'm asking for your help **so that** / **because of** what you have done in the past for our great city.

Please contact me if you have questions or if you'd like more information about our plan for a neighborhood watch.

Thank you,
Brenda Quinton
–Concerned citizen

4 Combine the phrases to make sentences. Add *although, because of, if, so,* or *so that*. Add a comma when necessary.

1. you should go to the health clinic / you don't feel well

   You should go to the health clinic if you don't feel well.

2. Dennis doesn't like sports / he plays basketball with his brother once in a while

   Although Dennis _____

3. Carla loves sports / she plays soccer and tennis at the recreation center

   _____

4. my mother enjoys being outside / she works a lot in the community garden

   _____

5. Mr. and Mrs. Quinton don't go out at night / the crime in the neighborhood

   _____

6. I'll go to the employment center tomorrow / I don't get this job today

   _____

7. we should ask for volunteers / the beautification project won't be too expensive

   _____

8. we have a great public library here / some people rarely read a book

   _____

5 Read the text. Then answer the questions.

> Neighbors! Although I'm happy that we have a new recycling center in the neighborhood, I think it needs to be improved. The containers aren't big enough, so there are always items on the floor. The area would be much cleaner if the containers were bigger. There is also no place to recycle newspapers, so I think that needs to be added. Someone told me the recycling center is small because of a lack of money. We need to write to Councilman Steven Sunders and tell him how important this center is so that something can be done about it. Neighbors – please help yourselves, and write a letter today so we can get this problem fixed! Email Shawn Davis for more information at SDavis@cup.com.

1. Is Shawn happy that there is a new recycling center?   Yes, he is.
2. Are the containers at the center big enough?   _____
3. Is the recycling center clean?   _____
4. What needs to be added to the center?   _____
5. Why is the recycling center small?   _____
6. Why does Shawn want people to write to Steven Sunders?   _____

D Getting involved

1 Read the text. What are three benefits of mobile health clinics?

They _____ 1 _____ , _____ 2 _____ , and _____ 3 _____ .

Health Clinics on the Move

Health care is a concern around the world. There are often too many people at hospitals, and in some areas people have to commute a long way to get to them. One solution to this problem is mobile health clinics. Mobile health clinics are like a small doctor's office in a van. The van drives to different locations so that people can get to it easily. Mobile clinics don't provide everything that a doctor's office or a hospital can, but there are a lot of services they do have. Doctors and nurses in mobile health clinics help people who are sick, test people for medical problems, and give patients information.

One benefit of mobile health clinics is that they can save money. When people are being checked at a mobile health clinic, they can avoid expensive trips to the emergency room. For example, in the United States, a trip to a mobile health clinic in Boston, Massachusetts, costs about $120. A visit to an emergency room in the same area is usually about $970.

Mobile health clinics can also help people avoid serious health problems. The St. Joseph Mobile Health Clinic in Santa Rosa, California, helps over 1,400 families every year. These are people who might not go to a doctor regularly if there weren't any mobile health clinics. They would only go to a hospital if they had serious problems. The mobile health clinic can catch problems before they get serious.

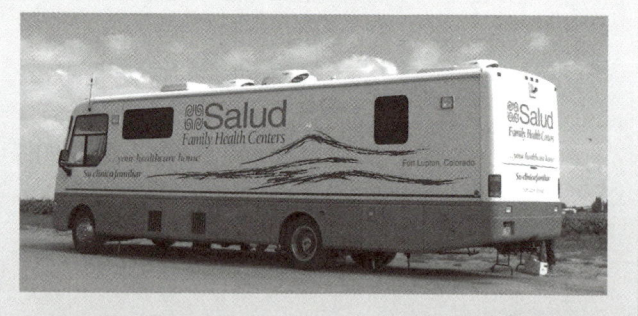

Mobile health clinics also bring care to people who don't live near medical services. For example, in Kenya, the clinics, hospitals, and doctors' offices are in large cities. So the mobile health clinics take the doctors and nurses to communities that are not near the large cities.

One program in Peru has mobile health clinics that include dental care. The program brings dentists to small communities with no dentists and educates people on how to take care of their teeth. Then they can keep their teeth healthy after the clinic leaves the area.

2 Read the text again. Then answer the questions.

1. What are three things doctors do in mobile health clinics? _help people who are sick, test people for medical problems, and give patients information_

2. How much does it cost to go to a mobile health clinic in Boston? _____

3. How many families go to the St. Joseph Mobile Clinic every year? _____

4. Why don't some people in Kenya go to doctors' offices or hospitals? _____

5. What is one kind of medical service provided by mobile clinics in Peru? _____